Filipino Americans

Nichol Bryan

ABDO
Publishing Company

visit us at
www.abdopub.com

Published by ABDO Publishing Company, 4940 Viking Drive, Edina, Minnesota 55435.
Copyright © 2004 by Abdo Consulting Group, Inc. International copyrights reserved in all
countries. No part of this book may be reproduced in any form without written permission from
the publisher.

Printed in the United States.

Cover Photo: Corbis
Interior Photos: AP/Wide World pp. 15, 21, 26, 27; Corbis pp. 1, 2-3, 5, 9, 14, 17, 23, 24,
    28, 30-31; Kayte Deioma pp. 19, 20, 25; TimePix pp. 13, 29

Editors: Kate A. Conley, Jennifer R. Krueger, Kristin Van Cleaf
Art Direction & Maps: Neil Klinepier

All of the U.S. population statistics in the One Nation series are taken from the 2000 Census.

Library of Congress Cataloging-in-Publication Data

Bryan, Nichol, 1958-
    Filipino Americans / Nichol Bryan.
        p. cm. -- (One nation)
    Includes index.
    Summary: Provides information on the history of the Philippines and on the customs,
language, religion, and experiences of Filipino Americans.
        ISBN 1-57765-988-0
        1. Filipino Americans--Juvenile literature. [1. Filipino Americans. 2. Immigrants.] I. Title.

E184.F4B79 2003
973'.09921--dc21

                                                                            2002043636

Contents

Filipino Americans

People of the Philippines have been making the voyage to the United States for more than 100 years. They chose this nation for the many opportunities it offered. America has long been known as a land of **immigrants**. In fact, most Americans today have ancestors who were born in other countries.

However, many Filipino immigrants have found that life in the United States isn't what they first expected. Finding jobs can be difficult, and many immigrants face **discrimination** from other Americans. Often, their children feel torn between their two **cultures**.

Immigrants are changed by their experiences in America. But, they change their new home as well. Today, the rich Filipino **heritage** is a part of America's culture. Filipino Americans help America continue to grow and change.

Opposite page: Filipino-American children

Philippine Past

The Philippines is an Asian country in the southwestern Pacific Ocean. The Philippines is a group of nearly 7,100 islands! For years, people have **emigrated** from these islands to other countries. They have left for different reasons throughout the country's history.

The Philippine Islands have been home to Filipino **culture** for hundreds of years. Starting in the mid-1500s, Spain controlled the Philippines. After the **Spanish-American War** of 1898, the United States took control of the islands. Under U.S. rule, Filipinos were considered U.S. **nationals**. That meant they could travel freely to the United States.

Beginning in the early 1900s, many Filipinos made this journey. They came to study or to find jobs. Many worked as farm laborers in Hawaii or California, or in fish canneries in Alaska. They sent money home to their families and hoped to someday return to the Philippines.

Then in the 1930s, the U.S. government changed its policies on the Philippines. The United States planned to give the Philippines its independence. That meant Filipinos were no longer considered **nationals**. **Immigration quotas** limited the number of Filipinos allowed to immigrate each year.

The Journey from the Philippines to the United States

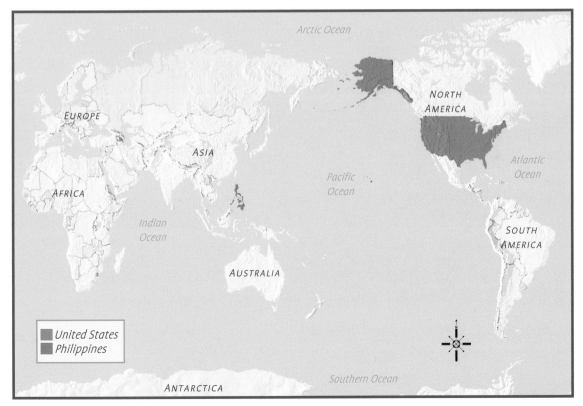

In 1946, after World War II, the United States granted the Philippines its independence. As a free country, the Philippines had to solve many problems. The **economy** was in bad shape, and many people had died in the war. The new government became **corrupt**, and **communist** rebels revolted in the 1950s.

During this difficult time, more Filipinos were making their way to the United States. New **immigration** laws allowed more Filipinos into the country. Other new laws allowed U.S. military officers to bring their wives and families over from the Philippines.

The Philippine government improved roads and schools in the late 1960s. The country still faced problems, however. In 1972, a corrupt president named Ferdinand Marcos declared **martial law**. It was about this time that many more Filipinos left the country. Many settled in the United States.

The Philippines continued to struggle. President Marcos was forced to flee in 1986, and Corazon Aquino became the country's first female president. However, the **economy** was still very weak and poverty was widespread. The government was almost overthrown a number of times. More and more Filipinos headed for the United States.

The Philippines is still troubled. **Corrupt** governments and revolts have hurt the country. Also, many of the big islands are crowded with the Philippines's 85 million people. It is hard for a poor country to provide for so many people.

Gloria Macapagal-Arroyo has been the Philippines's president since 2001.

For these reasons, many Filipinos have decided to become U.S. citizens. They still love the islands, but they see more opportunities for themselves and their children in America. Still, **immigrating** to the United States isn't always easy.

Challenges

Once they arrive in the United States, **immigrants** often encounter many challenges. It is not easy to come to a new country. Many Filipino immigrants had to leave behind their families. They were faced with finding a home, a job, and learning a **culture** different from their own.

Over the years, many Filipino immigrants entered the United States in Hawaii and California. Because of this, many Filipinos settled in those states. Los Angeles, California, for example, has a large Filipino-American community.

When Filipino immigrants first came to the United States in the early 1900s, they were often **discriminated** against. At a time when few Asians were allowed into the country, many Americans were fearful of Filipinos. Many of these early immigrants were uneducated and spoke little English. They were looked on as suspicious foreigners.

Some people thought Filipino immigrants were taking jobs away from other Americans. Because of this, Filipinos were often the

Filipino-American Communities

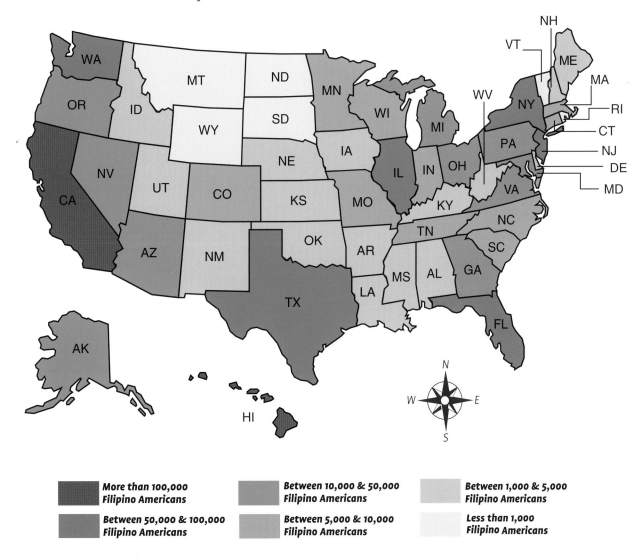

	More than 100,000 Filipino Americans		Between 10,000 & 50,000 Filipino Americans		Between 1,000 & 5,000 Filipino Americans
	Between 50,000 & 100,000 Filipino Americans		Between 5,000 & 10,000 Filipino Americans		Less than 1,000 Filipino Americans

targets of **racist** attacks, especially in the 1920s and 1930s. They were also **discriminated** against in public places, such as restaurants and hotels.

Laws kept Filipino **immigrants** from higher-paying jobs. A court case in the mid-1920s decided that, although Filipinos were U.S. **nationals**, they could not become citizens. Some jobs were reserved for citizens only. Many of the immigrants could find only low-wage jobs. What little money they earned was used for food and housing. This meant many had no money left to return to the Philippines, as they had originally hoped.

As time went on, other Americans became more accepting. Americans looked at Filipinos in a new light after many Filipinos helped fight in World War II. Around this time, Filipinos were allowed to become U.S. citizens. And, because many Filipino workers banded together in labor unions, they eventually gained better wages and treatment at work.

But, some discrimination continued. For example, in the 1970s more of the Filipinos coming to the United States were well educated. However, some Filipinos had trouble putting their education to use in the United States. It was not unusual to meet a Filipino-American college graduate with a low-paying job in a grocery or other retail store.

Early Filipino immigrants worked as farm laborers in places such as California and Hawaii.

Today, a larger range of jobs is open to Filipino Americans than in the past.

Filipino Americans still face some **discrimination** in the workplace. Some people are kept from getting better jobs because of their skin color or their accent. However, laws on equality have improved these situations. These laws, along with education, mean many recent Filipino **immigrants** have had an easier time than earlier immigrants in finding jobs that pay well.

Overall, Filipino immigrants today face different situations than in the past. Most recent Filipino immigrants already know a little about the United States, because it used to govern the Philippines. Even after independence, the United States had a large influence on the Philippines. This has made it easier for Filipino immigrants to adjust.

A network of help also exists in the Filipino-American community. Organizations offer different services to Filipino **immigrants**. Many Filipino Americans also lend a hand. There are even newspapers, books, and Web sites that give tips on topics such as job hunting. These resources make the move to the United States easier than it was for the first Filipino immigrants.

A Filipino American buys groceries from a Filipino store in California's Little Manila community.

Becoming a Citizen

Filipinos and other **immigrants** who come to the United States take the same path to citizenship. Immigrants become citizens in a process called naturalization. A government agency called the Immigration and Naturalization Service (INS) oversees this process.

The Path to Citizenship

Applying for Citizenship

The first step in becoming a citizen is filling out a form. It is called the Application for Naturalization. On the application, immigrants provide information about their past. Immigrants send the application to the INS.

Providing Information

Besides the application, immigrants must provide the INS with other items. They may include documents such as marriage licenses or old tax returns. Immigrants must also provide photographs and fingerprints. They are used for identification. The fingerprints are also used to check whether immigrants have committed crimes in the past.

The Interview

Next, an INS officer interviews each immigrant to discuss his or her application and background. In addition, the INS officer tests the immigrant's ability to speak, read, and write in English. The officer also tests the immigrant's knowledge of American civics.

The Oath

Immigrants approved for citizenship must take the Oath of Allegiance. Once immigrants take this oath, they are citizens. During the oath, immigrants promise to renounce loyalty to their native country, to support the U.S. Constitution, and to serve and defend the United States when needed.

Sample Questions from the Civics Test

How many stars are there on our flag?

What is the capital of the state you live in?

Why did the pilgrims come to America?

How many senators are there in Congress?

Who said, "Give me liberty or give me death"?

What are the first 10 amendments to the Constitution called?

In what month do we vote for the president?

Why Become a Citizen?

Why would an immigrant want to become a U.S. citizen? There are many reasons. Perhaps the biggest reason is that the U.S. Constitution grants many rights to its citizens. One of the most important is the right to vote.

U.S. Department of Justice
Immigration and Naturalization Service

Print clearly or type your answers using CAPITAL letters. Failure to print clearly may delay your application. Use bla

Application f

Part 1. Your Name *(The Person Applying for Naturalization)*

A. Your current legal name.

Family Name *(Last Name)*

Write your INS "A"- n

A _ _ _ _ _ _ _ _

Given Name *(First Name)*

Full Middle Name *(If applicable)*

FOR INS US

Bar Code

B. Your name exactly as it appears on your Permanent Resident Card.

Family Name *(Last Name)*

Given Name *(First Name)*

Full Middle Name *(If applicable)*

C. If you have ever used other names, provide them below.

Family Name *(Last Name)*

Given Name *(First Name)*

Middle Name

Filipino Culture

Filipino **culture** is a blend of different native cultures. But, it has also been shaped by Western influences. The Spanish introduced Catholicism, while the United States brought the English language. Filipino Americans often remember their background, while still blending into American society.

Family

A typical Filipino family consists of a father, mother, children, and other close relatives. Older family members are highly respected. Families often attend church and join other Filipino Americans in social activities. For example, weddings and birthdays are times for many Filipino Americans to socialize.

Some Filipino Americans send money back to relatives in the Philippines. For some, the money helps relatives live in their home country. Other Filipino Americans want their aunts, uncles, cousins, brothers, and sisters to join them in the United States. But, it can take years to save enough money to **emigrate**.

A Filipino-American mother and daughter make a parol, or star lantern.
Parols are traditional Christmas decorations in the Philippines.

Food

Filipino Americans eat many of the same foods as other Americans. However, some continue to make their traditional dishes. Traditional Filipino food often includes chicken, pork, and many tropical fruits. Cooks like to mix sweet and sour flavors, and different textures. These foods are often eaten with rice, a main food of the Philippines.

Dance

The Philippines's diverse **culture** is reflected in its many folk dances. Some of today's dances are based upon traditions of dancing for weddings, harvests, and other occasions. Others have Spanish influences or celebrate religious beliefs.

Two dancers perform the Pindulas. This is a wedding dance of the Yakan, a Muslim people of the southern Philippines.

Several Filipino dance troupes perform in different parts of the United States and the world to showcase their Filipino **heritage**. Folklorico Filipino Dance Company of New York and Likha Pilipino Folk Ensemble of San Francisco are two such dance companies.

Children begin a putong dance to welcome visitors at the opening of the Filipino Community Center in Honolulu, Hawaii.

Celebrations

Filipino communities often hold celebrations called fiestas. Fiestas are good places to see Filipino folk dances, paintings by Filipino-American artists, and performances by singers. Filipino Americans also hold festivals such as Flores de Mayo, a religious celebration.

A holiday honored by many Filipino Americans is the Philippines's Independence Day. One of the largest celebrations is held every year in New York on the first Sunday in June. A grand parade, a **cultural** show, and a street fair showcase Filipino culture.

Religion

Some Filipinos are Muslims, while others follow different religions. However, more than 90 percent of all Filipinos are Christian, and most are Roman Catholic. Saints are a central part of Catholic beliefs. One saint special to Filipinos is the Virgin of Antipolo.

Filipinos tell how in the 1600s, Spanish sailors gave a statue of the **Virgin Mary** to Catholic Filipinos. A few years later, the statue kept disappearing from its church and reappearing in a certain *tipolo* tree. The people decided to build a church there. They called the church Antipolo and put the statue in it. The statue eventually took on the name of the Virgin of Antipolo.

Devotions to the **Virgin Mary** have remained strong over the centuries. Filipino **immigrants** brought these beliefs to the United States. Recently, Catholic Filipino Americans created a shrine to the Virgin of Antipolo in Washington, D.C.

Filipino Americans celebrate many holidays, such as Philippine-American Friendship Day.

Language

People in the Philippine Islands speak around 70 closely related native languages and dialects. Their national language is Pilipino, which is similar to Tagalog, a common native language. However, most recent Filipino **immigrants** already know a lot of English when they arrive in the United States.

Many Filipino Americans are learning more about their heritage.

In the Philippine Islands, many students learn English. It is also used in shops and in the government. Filipinos may use some words differently than Americans do. But, knowing English makes adjusting to American society much easier.

Many Filipino **immigrants** also speak English at home with their children. They believe that this way, their children won't have an accent and may fit in better. But, this means many second-generation Filipino Americans grow up knowing little about their parents' **culture** and language.

A man at the Festival of Philippines Arts & Culture in San Pedro, California, displays gourds made into traditional hats.

Filipino Pride

Filipinos have brought with them a rich **culture**. They are known for their accomplishments in dance, in song, and in the arts. Filipinos are adding these traditions to America's cultural mix.

Art is an important part of Filipino-American culture. One of the most celebrated Filipino-American painters lived in New York. Venancio Igarta was a former farm worker who later created paintings bursting with color. Critics have called him a "Filipino genius."

Several Filipino Americans have also made names for themselves in music, including Lea Salonga. She is a singer and actress who has played parts in *Miss Saigon* and other Broadway and theater shows.

Lea Salonga played the role of Kim in Miss Saigon.

Another talented musician is country singer Neal McCoy. At first, no one believed he was a Filipino American. Because he dressed like a cowboy and had long, dark hair, they thought he was a Native American from the Southwest!

In the movies, a famous Filipino-American actor is Lou Diamond Phillips. He was born in the Philippines and grew up in Texas. He has starred in several successful movies, including *Courage Under Fire* and *Young Guns*. Another popular actor and comedian is Rob Schneider. He starred on *Saturday Night Live* and has also made several hit films.

Jessica Hagedorn

American literature has also benefited from Filipino talent. Jessica Hagedorn is a successful author of poems, novels, and plays. Hagedorn moved from the Philippines to San Francisco as a teenager. She started writing poetry and soon made a name for herself. She writes about the difficulties of being a part of multiple **cultures**.

Victoria Manalo Draves (center) after her victory in the 1948 Olympics

Filipino-American writing talent also extends to journalism. Byron Acohido and Alex Tizon each won a Pulitzer Prize for journalism in 1997. Another respected journalist is Howard Chua-Eoan. He has worked for *Time* magazine for nearly 20 years, and he became News Director in 2002.

Some Filipino Americans have been great athletes. Victoria Manalo Draves represented the United States in the 1948 Olympics. She was the first woman to win gold medals in both springboard and platform diving. Roman Gabriel was the first Filipino-American quarterback in the National Football League (NFL). He was named the NFL's Most Valuable Player in 1969.

These talented Filipino Americans are an important part of America's **culture**. In fact, nearly 2 million people of Philippine descent live in the United States today. Many young Filipino Americans are seeking out their roots. They are Americans, but feel a connection to the land their parents and grandparents left behind.

Howard Chua-Eoan

Glossary

communist - a person who supports communism. It is a social and economic system in which everything is owned by the government and is distributed to the people as needed.

corrupt - showing dishonest or improper behavior.

culture - the customs, arts, and tools of a nation or people at a certain time.

discrimination - unfair treatment based on factors such as a person's race, religion, or gender.

economy - the way a nation uses its money, goods, and natural resources.

emigration - to leave one's country and move to another. People who emigrate are called emigrants.

heritage - the handing down of something from one generation to the next.

immigration - entry into another country to live. People who immigrate are called immigrants.

martial law - law administered by government enforcement agencies, such as an army, when civilian enforcement agencies, such as police, can't maintain public order and safety.

national - a person who is under the protection of a nation, without the more formal recognition of citizenship.

quota - a limit to the number of people allowed to immigrate in a year. Immigration quotas are based on where a person is from.

racism - unfair treatment based on assumptions about a person's ethnic background.

Spanish-American War (1898) - a war between the United States and Spain that ended Spanish rule of Cuba, the Philippines, and other colonies.

Virgin Mary - the mother of Jesus.

Saying It

Byron Acohido - BY-run ah-koh-HEE-doh
Corazon Aquino - KAWR-ah-zon ah-KEE-no
fiesta - fee-EHS-tuh
Howard Chua-Eoan - HOW-urd CHOO-uh-EE-wahn
Philippines - fih-luh-PEENZ
Tagalog - tuh-GAH-lawg
Venancio Igarta - bay-NAHN-see-oh ee-GAHR-tah

Web Sites

To learn more about Filipino Americans, visit ABDO Publishing Company on the World Wide Web at **www.abdopub.com**. Web sites about Filipino Americans are featured on our Book Links page. These links are routinely monitored and updated to provide the most current information available.

31

Index